OUTTA THIS WORLD
SERMON NOTES FOR KIDS

PSALM 19:1 THE HEAVENS DECLARE THE
GLORY OF GOD; AND THE FIRMAMENT
SHEWETH HIS HANDYWORK.

this belongs to

WHO IS SPEAKING?

DATE: / /

FAVORITE SONG THAT
WAS SUNG TODAY:

DRAW SOMETHING FROM TODAY'S BIBLE STORY

WHAT WAS THE SERMON ABOUT?

SOMETHING I'D LIKE TO PRAY FOR:

WORDS I HEARD BUT DIDN'T UNDERSTAND:

ONE THING GOD'S WORD TAUGHT ME TODAY:

A DECISION I MADE FOR THE LORD:

QUESTIONS I HAVE:

WHO IS SPEAKING?

DATE: /   /

FAVORITE SONG THAT
WAS SUNG TODAY:

DRAW SOMETHING FROM TODAY'S BIBLE STORY

WHAT WAS THE SERMON ABOUT?

SOMETHING I'D LIKE TO PRAY FOR:

WORDS I HEARD BUT
DIDN'T UNDERSTAND:

ONE THING GOD'S WORD
TAUGHT ME TODAY:

A DECISION I MADE FOR THE LORD:

QUESTIONS I HAVE:

WHO IS SPEAKING?

DATE: / /

FAVORITE SONG THAT
WAS SUNG TODAY:

DRAW SOMETHING FROM TODAY'S BIBLE STORY

WHAT WAS THE SERMON ABOUT?

SOMETHING I'D LIKE TO PRAY FOR:

WORDS I HEARD BUT DIDN'T UNDERSTAND:

ONE THING GOD'S WORD TAUGHT ME TODAY:

A DECISION I MADE FOR THE LORD:

QUESTIONS I HAVE:

WHO IS SPEAKING?

DATE: / /

FAVORITE SONG THAT
WAS SUNG TODAY:

DRAW SOMETHING FROM TODAY'S BIBLE STORY

WHAT WAS THE SERMON ABOUT?

SOMETHING I'D LIKE TO PRAY FOR:

WORDS I HEARD BUT
DIDN'T UNDERSTAND:

ONE THING GOD'S WORD
TAUGHT ME TODAY:

A DECISION I MADE FOR THE LORD:

QUESTIONS I HAVE:

WHO IS SPEAKING?

DATE: /   /

FAVORITE SONG THAT
WAS SUNG TODAY:

DRAW SOMETHING FROM TODAY'S BIBLE STORY

WHAT WAS THE SERMON ABOUT?

SOMETHING I'D LIKE TO PRAY FOR:

WORDS I HEARD BUT
DIDN'T UNDERSTAND:

ONE THING GOD'S WORD
TAUGHT ME TODAY:

A DECISION I MADE FOR THE LORD:

QUESTIONS I HAVE:

WHO IS SPEAKING?

DATE: _____ / _____ / _____

FAVORITE SONG THAT
WAS SUNG TODAY:

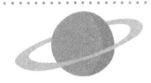

DRAW SOMETHING FROM TODAY'S BIBLE STORY

WHAT WAS THE SERMON ABOUT?

SOMETHING I'D LIKE TO PRAY FOR:

WORDS I HEARD BUT DIDN'T UNDERSTAND:

ONE THING GOD'S WORD TAUGHT ME TODAY:

A DECISION I MADE FOR THE LORD:

QUESTIONS I HAVE:

WHO IS SPEAKING?

DATE: / /

FAVORITE SONG THAT
WAS SUNG TODAY:

DRAW SOMETHING FROM TODAY'S BIBLE STORY

WHAT WAS THE SERMON ABOUT?

SOMETHING I'D LIKE TO PRAY FOR:

WORDS I HEARD BUT
DIDN'T UNDERSTAND:

ONE THING GOD'S WORD
TAUGHT ME TODAY:

A DECISION I MADE FOR THE LORD:

QUESTIONS I HAVE:

WHO IS SPEAKING?

DATE: /   /

FAVORITE SONG THAT
WAS SUNG TODAY:

DRAW SOMETHING FROM TODAY'S BIBLE STORY

WHAT WAS THE SERMON ABOUT?

SOMETHING I'D LIKE TO PRAY FOR:

WORDS I HEARD BUT
DIDN'T UNDERSTAND:

ONE THING GOD'S WORD
TAUGHT ME TODAY:

A DECISION I MADE FOR THE LORD:

QUESTIONS I HAVE:

WHO IS SPEAKING?

DATE: / /

FAVORITE SONG THAT
WAS SUNG TODAY:

DRAW SOMETHING FROM TODAY'S BIBLE STORY

WHAT WAS THE SERMON ABOUT?

SOMETHING I'D LIKE TO PRAY FOR:

WORDS I HEARD BUT
DIDN'T UNDERSTAND:

ONE THING GOD'S WORD
TAUGHT ME TODAY:

A DECISION I MADE FOR THE LORD:

QUESTIONS I HAVE:

WHO IS SPEAKING?

DATE: / /

FAVORITE SONG THAT WAS SUNG TODAY:

DRAW SOMETHING FROM TODAY'S BIBLE STORY

WHAT WAS THE SERMON ABOUT?

SOMETHING I'D LIKE TO PRAY FOR:

WORDS I HEARD BUT
DIDN'T UNDERSTAND:

ONE THING GOD'S WORD
TAUGHT ME TODAY:

A DECISION I MADE FOR THE LORD:

QUESTIONS I HAVE:

WHO IS SPEAKING?

DATE: ___ / ___ / ___

FAVORITE SONG THAT
WAS SUNG TODAY:

DRAW SOMETHING FROM TODAY'S BIBLE STORY

WHAT WAS THE SERMON ABOUT?

SOMETHING I'D LIKE TO PRAY FOR:

WORDS I HEARD BUT
DIDN'T UNDERSTAND:

ONE THING GOD'S WORD
TAUGHT ME TODAY:

A DECISION I MADE FOR THE LORD:

QUESTIONS I HAVE:

WHO IS SPEAKING?

DATE: / /

FAVORITE SONG THAT
WAS SUNG TODAY:

DRAW SOMETHING FROM TODAY'S BIBLE STORY

WHAT WAS THE SERMON ABOUT?

SOMETHING I'D LIKE TO PRAY FOR:

WORDS I HEARD BUT DIDN'T UNDERSTAND:

ONE THING GOD'S WORD TAUGHT ME TODAY:

A DECISION I MADE FOR THE LORD:

QUESTIONS I HAVE:

WHO IS SPEAKING?

DATE: / /

FAVORITE SONG THAT
WAS SUNG TODAY:

DRAW SOMETHING FROM TODAY'S BIBLE STORY

WHAT WAS THE SERMON ABOUT?

SOMETHING I'D LIKE TO PRAY FOR:

WORDS I HEARD BUT DIDN'T UNDERSTAND:

ONE THING GOD'S WORD TAUGHT ME TODAY:

A DECISION I MADE FOR THE LORD:

QUESTIONS I HAVE:

WHO IS SPEAKING?

DATE: _____ / _____ / _____

FAVORITE SONG THAT
WAS SUNG TODAY:

DRAW SOMETHING FROM TODAY'S BIBLE STORY

WHAT WAS THE SERMON ABOUT?

SOMETHING I'D LIKE TO PRAY FOR:

WORDS I HEARD BUT
DIDN'T UNDERSTAND:

ONE THING GOD'S WORD
TAUGHT ME TODAY:

A DECISION I MADE FOR THE LORD:

QUESTIONS I HAVE:

WHO IS SPEAKING?

DATE: / /

FAVORITE SONG THAT
WAS SUNG TODAY:

DRAW SOMETHING FROM TODAY'S BIBLE STORY

WHAT WAS THE SERMON ABOUT?

SOMETHING I'D LIKE TO PRAY FOR:

WORDS I HEARD BUT DIDN'T UNDERSTAND:

ONE THING GOD'S WORD TAUGHT ME TODAY:

A DECISION I MADE FOR THE LORD:

QUESTIONS I HAVE:

WHO IS SPEAKING?

DATE: / /

FAVORITE SONG THAT
WAS SUNG TODAY:

DRAW SOMETHING FROM TODAY'S BIBLE STORY

WHAT WAS THE SERMON ABOUT?

SOMETHING I'D LIKE TO PRAY FOR:

WORDS I HEARD BUT
DIDN'T UNDERSTAND:

ONE THING GOD'S WORD
TAUGHT ME TODAY:

A DECISION I MADE FOR THE LORD:

QUESTIONS I HAVE:

WHO IS SPEAKING?

FAVORITE SONG THAT
WAS SUNG TODAY:

DRAW SOMETHING FROM TODAY'S BIBLE STORY

WHAT WAS THE SERMON ABOUT?

SOMETHING I'D LIKE TO PRAY FOR:

WORDS I HEARD BUT DIDN'T UNDERSTAND:

ONE THING GOD'S WORD TAUGHT ME TODAY:

A DECISION I MADE FOR THE LORD:

QUESTIONS I HAVE:

WHO IS SPEAKING?

DATE: / /

FAVORITE SONG THAT
WAS SUNG TODAY:

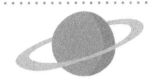

DRAW SOMETHING FROM TODAY'S BIBLE STORY

WHAT WAS THE SERMON ABOUT?

SOMETHING I'D LIKE TO PRAY FOR:

WORDS I HEARD BUT
DIDN'T UNDERSTAND:

ONE THING GOD'S WORD
TAUGHT ME TODAY:

A DECISION I MADE FOR THE LORD:

QUESTIONS I HAVE:

WHO IS SPEAKING?

DATE: /   /

FAVORITE SONG THAT
WAS SUNG TODAY:

DRAW SOMETHING FROM TODAY'S BIBLE STORY

WHAT WAS THE SERMON ABOUT?

SOMETHING I'D LIKE TO PRAY FOR:

WORDS I HEARD BUT DIDN'T UNDERSTAND:

ONE THING GOD'S WORD TAUGHT ME TODAY:

A DECISION I MADE FOR THE LORD:

QUESTIONS I HAVE:

WHO IS SPEAKING?

DATE: / /

FAVORITE SONG THAT
WAS SUNG TODAY:

DRAW SOMETHING FROM TODAY'S BIBLE STORY

WHAT WAS THE SERMON ABOUT?

SOMETHING I'D LIKE TO PRAY FOR:

WORDS I HEARD BUT DIDN'T UNDERSTAND:

ONE THING GOD'S WORD TAUGHT ME TODAY:

A DECISION I MADE FOR THE LORD:

QUESTIONS I HAVE:

WHO IS SPEAKING?

DATE: /   /

FAVORITE SONG THAT
WAS SUNG TODAY:

DRAW SOMETHING FROM TODAY'S BIBLE STORY

WHAT WAS THE SERMON ABOUT?

SOMETHING I'D LIKE TO PRAY FOR:

WORDS I HEARD BUT
DIDN'T UNDERSTAND:

ONE THING GOD'S WORD
TAUGHT ME TODAY:

A DECISION I MADE FOR THE LORD:

QUESTIONS I HAVE:

WHO IS SPEAKING?

DATE: / /

FAVORITE SONG THAT
WAS SUNG TODAY:

DRAW SOMETHING FROM TODAY'S BIBLE STORY

WHAT WAS THE SERMON ABOUT?

SOMETHING I'D LIKE TO PRAY FOR:

WORDS I HEARD BUT
DIDN'T UNDERSTAND:

ONE THING GOD'S WORD
TAUGHT ME TODAY:

A DECISION I MADE FOR THE LORD:

QUESTIONS I HAVE:

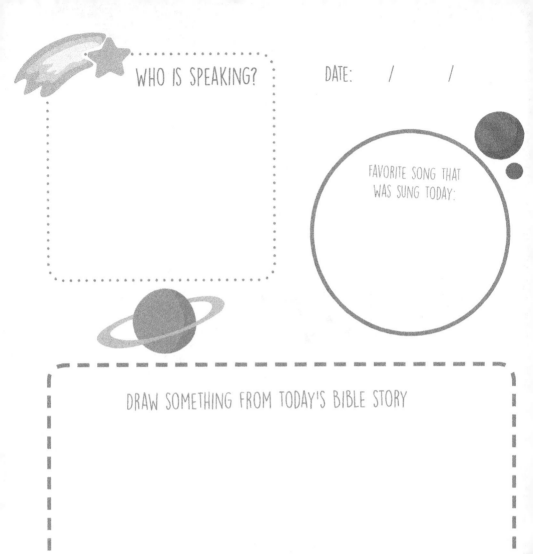

WHO IS SPEAKING?

DATE: / /

FAVORITE SONG THAT
WAS SUNG TODAY:

DRAW SOMETHING FROM TODAY'S BIBLE STORY

WHAT WAS THE SERMON ABOUT?

SOMETHING I'D LIKE TO PRAY FOR:

WORDS I HEARD BUT
DIDN'T UNDERSTAND:

ONE THING GOD'S WORD
TAUGHT ME TODAY:

A DECISION I MADE FOR THE LORD:

QUESTIONS I HAVE:

WHO IS SPEAKING?

DATE: / /

FAVORITE SONG THAT WAS SUNG TODAY:

DRAW SOMETHING FROM TODAY'S BIBLE STORY

WHAT WAS THE SERMON ABOUT?

SOMETHING I'D LIKE TO PRAY FOR:

WORDS I HEARD BUT DIDN'T UNDERSTAND:

ONE THING GOD'S WORD TAUGHT ME TODAY:

A DECISION I MADE FOR THE LORD:

QUESTIONS I HAVE:

WHO IS SPEAKING?

DATE: / /

FAVORITE SONG THAT
WAS SUNG TODAY:

DRAW SOMETHING FROM TODAY'S BIBLE STORY

WHAT WAS THE SERMON ABOUT?

SOMETHING I'D LIKE TO PRAY FOR:

WORDS I HEARD BUT
DIDN'T UNDERSTAND:

ONE THING GOD'S WORD
TAUGHT ME TODAY:

A DECISION I MADE FOR THE LORD:

QUESTIONS I HAVE:

WHO IS SPEAKING?

DATE: ___ / ___ / ___

FAVORITE SONG THAT
WAS SUNG TODAY:

DRAW SOMETHING FROM TODAY'S BIBLE STORY

WHAT WAS THE SERMON ABOUT?

SOMETHING I'D LIKE TO PRAY FOR:

WORDS I HEARD BUT DIDN'T UNDERSTAND:

ONE THING GOD'S WORD TAUGHT ME TODAY:

A DECISION I MADE FOR THE LORD:

QUESTIONS I HAVE:

WHO IS SPEAKING?

DATE: / /

FAVORITE SONG THAT
WAS SUNG TODAY:

DRAW SOMETHING FROM TODAY'S BIBLE STORY

WHAT WAS THE SERMON ABOUT?

SOMETHING I'D LIKE TO PRAY FOR:

WORDS I HEARD BUT DIDN'T UNDERSTAND:

ONE THING GOD'S WORD TAUGHT ME TODAY:

A DECISION I MADE FOR THE LORD:

QUESTIONS I HAVE:

WHO IS SPEAKING?

DATE: / /

FAVORITE SONG THAT
WAS SUNG TODAY:

DRAW SOMETHING FROM TODAY'S BIBLE STORY

WHAT WAS THE SERMON ABOUT?

SOMETHING I'D LIKE TO PRAY FOR:

WORDS I HEARD BUT
DIDN'T UNDERSTAND:

ONE THING GOD'S WORD
TAUGHT ME TODAY:

A DECISION I MADE FOR THE LORD:

QUESTIONS I HAVE:

WHO IS SPEAKING?

DATE: /   /

FAVORITE SONG THAT
WAS SUNG TODAY:

DRAW SOMETHING FROM TODAY'S BIBLE STORY

WHAT WAS THE SERMON ABOUT?

SOMETHING I'D LIKE TO PRAY FOR:

WORDS I HEARD BUT
DIDN'T UNDERSTAND:

ONE THING GOD'S WORD
TAUGHT ME TODAY:

A DECISION I MADE FOR THE LORD:

QUESTIONS I HAVE:

WHO IS SPEAKING?

DATE: / /

FAVORITE SONG THAT
WAS SUNG TODAY:

DRAW SOMETHING FROM TODAY'S BIBLE STORY

WHAT WAS THE SERMON ABOUT?

SOMETHING I'D LIKE TO PRAY FOR:

WORDS I HEARD BUT
DIDN'T UNDERSTAND:

ONE THING GOD'S WORD
TAUGHT ME TODAY:

A DECISION I MADE FOR THE LORD:

QUESTIONS I HAVE:

WHO IS SPEAKING?

DATE: /   /

FAVORITE SONG THAT
WAS SUNG TODAY:

DRAW SOMETHING FROM TODAY'S BIBLE STORY

WHAT WAS THE SERMON ABOUT?

SOMETHING I'D LIKE TO PRAY FOR:

WORDS I HEARD BUT
DIDN'T UNDERSTAND:

ONE THING GOD'S WORD
TAUGHT ME TODAY:

A DECISION I MADE FOR THE LORD:

QUESTIONS I HAVE:

WHO IS SPEAKING?

DATE: / /

FAVORITE SONG THAT
WAS SUNG TODAY:

DRAW SOMETHING FROM TODAY'S BIBLE STORY

WHAT WAS THE SERMON ABOUT?

SOMETHING I'D LIKE TO PRAY FOR:

WORDS I HEARD BUT
DIDN'T UNDERSTAND:

ONE THING GOD'S WORD
TAUGHT ME TODAY:

A DECISION I MADE FOR THE LORD:

QUESTIONS I HAVE:

WHO IS SPEAKING?

DATE: /   /

FAVORITE SONG THAT
WAS SUNG TODAY:

DRAW SOMETHING FROM TODAY'S BIBLE STORY

WHAT WAS THE SERMON ABOUT?

SOMETHING I'D LIKE TO PRAY FOR:

WORDS I HEARD BUT
DIDN'T UNDERSTAND:

ONE THING GOD'S WORD
TAUGHT ME TODAY:

A DECISION I MADE FOR THE LORD:

QUESTIONS I HAVE:

WHO IS SPEAKING?

DATE: /   /

FAVORITE SONG THAT
WAS SUNG TODAY:

DRAW SOMETHING FROM TODAY'S BIBLE STORY

WHAT WAS THE SERMON ABOUT?

SOMETHING I'D LIKE TO PRAY FOR:

WORDS I HEARD BUT
DIDN'T UNDERSTAND:

ONE THING GOD'S WORD
TAUGHT ME TODAY:

A DECISION I MADE FOR THE LORD:

QUESTIONS I HAVE:

WHO IS SPEAKING?

DATE: /   /

FAVORITE SONG THAT
WAS SUNG TODAY:

DRAW SOMETHING FROM TODAY'S BIBLE STORY

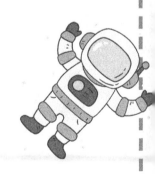

WHAT WAS THE SERMON ABOUT?

SOMETHING I'D LIKE TO PRAY FOR:

WORDS I HEARD BUT DIDN'T UNDERSTAND:

ONE THING GOD'S WORD TAUGHT ME TODAY:

A DECISION I MADE FOR THE LORD:

QUESTIONS I HAVE:

WHO IS SPEAKING?

DATE: / /

FAVORITE SONG THAT
WAS SUNG TODAY:

DRAW SOMETHING FROM TODAY'S BIBLE STORY

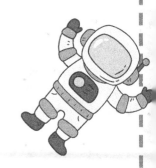

WHAT WAS THE SERMON ABOUT?

SOMETHING I'D LIKE TO PRAY FOR:

WORDS I HEARD BUT DIDN'T UNDERSTAND:

ONE THING GOD'S WORD TAUGHT ME TODAY:

A DECISION I MADE FOR THE LORD:

QUESTIONS I HAVE:

WHO IS SPEAKING?

DATE: ___/___/___

FAVORITE SONG THAT
WAS SUNG TODAY:

DRAW SOMETHING FROM TODAY'S BIBLE STORY

WHAT WAS THE SERMON ABOUT?

SOMETHING I'D LIKE TO PRAY FOR:

WORDS I HEARD BUT DIDN'T UNDERSTAND:

ONE THING GOD'S WORD TAUGHT ME TODAY:

A DECISION I MADE FOR THE LORD:

QUESTIONS I HAVE:

WHO IS SPEAKING?

DATE: / /

FAVORITE SONG THAT
WAS SUNG TODAY:

DRAW SOMETHING FROM TODAY'S BIBLE STORY

WHAT WAS THE SERMON ABOUT?

SOMETHING I'D LIKE TO PRAY FOR:

WORDS I HEARD BUT DIDN'T UNDERSTAND:

ONE THING GOD'S WORD TAUGHT ME TODAY:

A DECISION I MADE FOR THE LORD:

QUESTIONS I HAVE:

WHO IS SPEAKING?

DATE: /   /

FAVORITE SONG THAT
WAS SUNG TODAY:

DRAW SOMETHING FROM TODAY'S BIBLE STORY

WHAT WAS THE SERMON ABOUT?

SOMETHING I'D LIKE TO PRAY FOR:

WORDS I HEARD BUT
DIDN'T UNDERSTAND:

ONE THING GOD'S WORD
TAUGHT ME TODAY:

A DECISION I MADE FOR THE LORD:

QUESTIONS I HAVE:

WHO IS SPEAKING?

DATE: / /

FAVORITE SONG THAT WAS SUNG TODAY:

DRAW SOMETHING FROM TODAY'S BIBLE STORY

WHAT WAS THE SERMON ABOUT?

SOMETHING I'D LIKE TO PRAY FOR:

WORDS I HEARD BUT DIDN'T UNDERSTAND:

ONE THING GOD'S WORD TAUGHT ME TODAY:

A DECISION I MADE FOR THE LORD:

QUESTIONS I HAVE:

WHO IS SPEAKING?

DATE: /   /

FAVORITE SONG THAT
WAS SUNG TODAY:

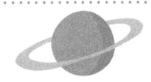

DRAW SOMETHING FROM TODAY'S BIBLE STORY

WHAT WAS THE SERMON ABOUT?

SOMETHING I'D LIKE TO PRAY FOR:

WORDS I HEARD BUT DIDN'T UNDERSTAND:

ONE THING GOD'S WORD TAUGHT ME TODAY:

A DECISION I MADE FOR THE LORD:

QUESTIONS I HAVE:

WHO IS SPEAKING?

DATE: / /

FAVORITE SONG THAT
WAS SUNG TODAY:

DRAW SOMETHING FROM TODAY'S BIBLE STORY

WHAT WAS THE SERMON ABOUT?

SOMETHING I'D LIKE TO PRAY FOR:

WORDS I HEARD BUT
DIDN'T UNDERSTAND:

ONE THING GOD'S WORD
TAUGHT ME TODAY:

A DECISION I MADE FOR THE LORD:

QUESTIONS I HAVE:

WHO IS SPEAKING?

DATE: /   /

FAVORITE SONG THAT
WAS SUNG TODAY:

DRAW SOMETHING FROM TODAY'S BIBLE STORY

WHAT WAS THE SERMON ABOUT?

SOMETHING I'D LIKE TO PRAY FOR:

WORDS I HEARD BUT
DIDN'T UNDERSTAND:

ONE THING GOD'S WORD
TAUGHT ME TODAY:

A DECISION I MADE FOR THE LORD:

QUESTIONS I HAVE:

WHO IS SPEAKING?

DATE: /   /

FAVORITE SONG THAT
WAS SUNG TODAY:

DRAW SOMETHING FROM TODAY'S BIBLE STORY

WHAT WAS THE SERMON ABOUT?

SOMETHING I'D LIKE TO PRAY FOR:

WORDS I HEARD BUT
DIDN'T UNDERSTAND:

ONE THING GOD'S WORD
TAUGHT ME TODAY:

A DECISION I MADE FOR THE LORD:

QUESTIONS I HAVE:

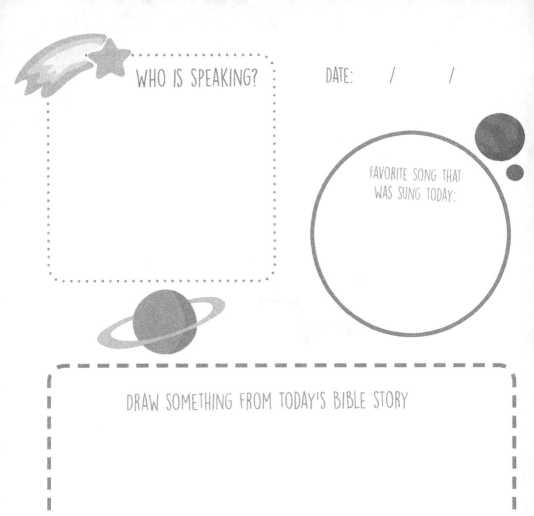

WHO IS SPEAKING?

DATE: / /

FAVORITE SONG THAT WAS SUNG TODAY:

DRAW SOMETHING FROM TODAY'S BIBLE STORY

WHAT WAS THE SERMON ABOUT?

SOMETHING I'D LIKE TO PRAY FOR:

WORDS I HEARD BUT
DIDN'T UNDERSTAND:

ONE THING GOD'S WORD
TAUGHT ME TODAY:

A DECISION I MADE FOR THE LORD:

QUESTIONS I HAVE:

WHO IS SPEAKING?

DATE: / /

FAVORITE SONG THAT
WAS SUNG TODAY:

DRAW SOMETHING FROM TODAY'S BIBLE STORY

WHAT WAS THE SERMON ABOUT?

SOMETHING I'D LIKE TO PRAY FOR:

WORDS I HEARD BUT DIDN'T UNDERSTAND:

ONE THING GOD'S WORD TAUGHT ME TODAY:

A DECISION I MADE FOR THE LORD:

QUESTIONS I HAVE:

WHO IS SPEAKING?

DATE: ___ / ___ / ___

FAVORITE SONG THAT
WAS SUNG TODAY:

DRAW SOMETHING FROM TODAY'S BIBLE STORY

WHAT WAS THE SERMON ABOUT?

SOMETHING I'D LIKE TO PRAY FOR:

WORDS I HEARD BUT
DIDN'T UNDERSTAND:

ONE THING GOD'S WORD
TAUGHT ME TODAY:

A DECISION I MADE FOR THE LORD:

QUESTIONS I HAVE:

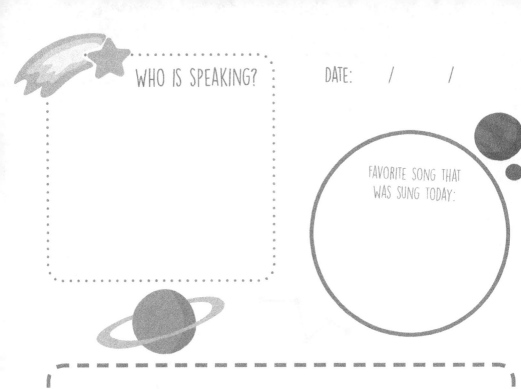

WHO IS SPEAKING?

DATE: / /

FAVORITE SONG THAT
WAS SUNG TODAY:

DRAW SOMETHING FROM TODAY'S BIBLE STORY

WHAT WAS THE SERMON ABOUT?

SOMETHING I'D LIKE TO PRAY FOR:

WORDS I HEARD BUT DIDN'T UNDERSTAND:

ONE THING GOD'S WORD TAUGHT ME TODAY:

A DECISION I MADE FOR THE LORD:

QUESTIONS I HAVE:

WHO IS SPEAKING?

DATE: / /

FAVORITE SONG THAT
WAS SUNG TODAY:

DRAW SOMETHING FROM TODAY'S BIBLE STORY

WHAT WAS THE SERMON ABOUT?

SOMETHING I'D LIKE TO PRAY FOR:

WORDS I HEARD BUT DIDN'T UNDERSTAND:

ONE THING GOD'S WORD TAUGHT ME TODAY:

A DECISION I MADE FOR THE LORD:

QUESTIONS I HAVE:

WHO IS SPEAKING?

DATE: / /

FAVORITE SONG THAT
WAS SUNG TODAY:

DRAW SOMETHING FROM TODAY'S BIBLE STORY

WHAT WAS THE SERMON ABOUT?

SOMETHING I'D LIKE TO PRAY FOR:

WORDS I HEARD BUT DIDN'T UNDERSTAND:

ONE THING GOD'S WORD TAUGHT ME TODAY:

A DECISION I MADE FOR THE LORD:

QUESTIONS I HAVE:

WHO IS SPEAKING?

DATE: / /

FAVORITE SONG THAT
WAS SUNG TODAY:

DRAW SOMETHING FROM TODAY'S BIBLE STORY

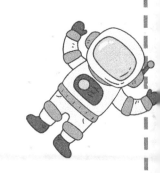

WHAT WAS THE SERMON ABOUT?

SOMETHING I'D LIKE TO PRAY FOR:

WORDS I HEARD BUT
DIDN'T UNDERSTAND:

ONE THING GOD'S WORD
TAUGHT ME TODAY:

A DECISION I MADE FOR THE LORD:

QUESTIONS I HAVE:

WHO IS SPEAKING?

DATE: / /

FAVORITE SONG THAT
WAS SUNG TODAY:

DRAW SOMETHING FROM TODAY'S BIBLE STORY

WHAT WAS THE SERMON ABOUT?

SOMETHING I'D LIKE TO PRAY FOR:

WORDS I HEARD BUT
DIDN'T UNDERSTAND:

ONE THING GOD'S WORD
TAUGHT ME TODAY:

A DECISION I MADE FOR THE LORD:

QUESTIONS I HAVE:

To order more copies and to see a variety of styles
available go to Amazon.com and search for
Family Closet Treasures Sermon Notes

CPSIA information can be obtained
at www.ICGtesting.com
Printed in the USA
LVHW040916151019
634129LV00021B/3099/P

9 781696 975926